Asus ROG Ally X User Guide

**Exploring a Detailed Guide
Customization and Features**

Linda B. Jordan

Copyright

Table of Contents

Initial Setup and Configuration
Connecting to Wi-Fi and Microsoft Account Setup
Windows 11 Installation and Settings Overview
Updating Firmware and Drivers
Installing ASUS Armoury Crate Software

4. Customizing the ROG Ally X
RGB Lighting Customization
Button Remapping and Profiles
Adjusting Display Settings (Resolution, Refresh Rate)
Audio Settings and Headphone Configuration

5. Navigating Windows 11 on ROG Ally X
Using Windows 11 on a Handheld Console
Switching Between Handheld Mode and Desktop Mode
Desktop Shortcuts for Quick Access
Setting Up External Monitors and eGPU

6. Gaming on the ROG Ally X
Installing and Running Games (Steam, Epic, GOG, etc.)
Performance Modes for Optimized Gaming
Adjusting In-Game Settings for Better Performance
Using Armoury Crate for Game Customization
Managing Game Libraries and External Storage
Using the MicroSD Slot
Expanding Internal Storage (SSD Upgrade Guide)

7. Emulation on the ROG Ally X
Installing Emulators
Running Retro Games
Recommended Emulator Settings and Tools

Introduction

Welcome to the ASUS ROG Ally X, the latest evolution in handheld gaming technology. This powerful device is designed for gamers who want the performance of a PC in a portable form factor, allowing you to enjoy high-quality gaming experiences anywhere, anytime. Whether you're a casual gamer or a dedicated enthusiast, the ROG Ally X brings the cutting-edge performance and customization options you need to elevate your gaming sessions.

Building on the foundation of its predecessor, the original ASUS ROG Ally, the ROG Ally X pushes the boundaries of what's possible in a handheld gaming console. It blends PC-level gaming performance with console-like portability, offering users a sleek and ergonomic design packed with powerful hardware that can run the latest AAA games and indie titles alike.

With the ROG Ally X, ASUS has responded to the demands of gamers by improving battery life, increasing storage options, and refining the controls for an enhanced gaming experience. This device is designed for users who want to play heavy, high-performance games on the go without sacrificing the visual and performance quality typically associated with desktop PCs or larger gaming consoles. Whether you're on the train, at a café, or just relaxing at home, the ROG Ally X ensures you can game seamlessly, wherever life takes you.

Key Features Overview:

The ASUS ROG Ally X is packed with a range of impressive features that make it stand out from other handheld gaming devices. Let's explore some of its key attributes:

1. Powerful AMD Ryzen Z1 Extreme Processor

At the heart of the ROG Ally X is the AMD Ryzen Z1 Extreme chip, delivering desktop-level performance in a portable format. This CPU is optimized for gaming, ensuring smooth performance across a wide range of titles, from AAA blockbusters to indie gems.

2. 24GB of LPDDR5X RAM

With 24GB of ultra-fast LPDDR5X RAM, the ROG Ally X offers enough memory to handle even the most resource-demanding games. The high-frequency RAM ensures faster load times, smoother multitasking, and better overall gaming performance.

3. 1TB SSD Storage (Upgradeable)

The ROG Ally X comes with 1TB of onboard SSD storage, providing ample space for your game library, media, and apps. The device also supports storage upgrades, allowing users to swap out the SSD for up to 8TB of additional space if needed.

4. 7-Inch 1080p 120Hz Display

Enjoy stunning visuals on the 7-inch Full HD (1080p) display with a 120Hz refresh rate. This high refresh rate ensures fluid animations and reduces motion blur, delivering an immersive gaming experience. The 1080p resolution provides crisp visuals, though it's not OLED—an area where ASUS prioritizes refresh rate and performance over display technology.

5. Extended Battery Life (80Wh)

One of the standout improvements over the previous generation is the 80Wh battery, which doubles the battery capacity of the original ROG Ally. This allows for extended gaming sessions without the need to recharge constantly. Depending on usage and power settings, the Ally X can last for up to 3-5 hours unplugged, giving you ample time to enjoy your favorite games.

6. Ergonomic Design and Durable Build

The ROG Ally X has been designed with ergonomics in mind, ensuring a comfortable grip during long gaming sessions. Its lightweight build and contoured body fit snugly in your hands, with offset analog sticks that mimic the layout of an Xbox controller, offering improved comfort and control. The buttons are tactile, the triggers have been enhanced, and the concave joysticks are built to last, supporting up to five million cycles.

7. Upgraded Cooling System

Keeping the powerful internals cool is a priority, and the upgraded cooling system on the ROG Ally X does just that. With a stronger fan and improved heat dissipation, the console can handle longer gaming sessions without overheating. The cooling system is quieter and more efficient, ensuring that your device remains cool without producing excessive noise.

8. RGB Customization

The Ally X features customizable RGB lighting for added flair. Users can personalize the RGB zones to match their gaming setup or mood, creating a unique and dynamic look while gaming.

9. Windows 11 Compatibility

Unlike other handheld consoles that run on proprietary operating systems, the ROG Ally X runs on Windows 11, providing a full-fledged PC experience. This means you can access not just your game libraries from platforms like Steam,

Epic Games, and Xbox Game Pass, but also use standard PC applications like browsers, productivity tools, and media players.

10. Dual USB-C Ports and eGPU Support

The inclusion of two USB-C ports (one USB4) allows for versatile connectivity. You can charge your device while simultaneously connecting to external peripherals or an external GPU (eGPU) to boost your gaming performance when playing at home. This makes the ROG Ally X a hybrid device, capable of functioning as both a handheld console and a powerful desktop gaming machine when docked with an eGPU.

Box Contents:

Upon unboxing your ASUS ROG Ally X, you'll find the following components carefully packed:

1. ROG Ally X Console

The main device features all the power and performance you need for gaming on the go.

2. 65W USB-C Power Adapter

A compact power adapter designed for fast charging, ensuring that you can recharge your device quickly and get back into the game.

3. USB-C to USB-C Charging Cable

A durable cable for connecting the power adapter to the console. It supports high-speed charging and data transfer.

4. Quick Start Guide

A user manual that provides an overview of how to set up your device, basic operations, and safety guidelines.

5. Warranty Card

Important documentation covering the warranty period and information on how to claim repairs or replacements if necessary.

6. Optional Accessories (Depending on Package)

Some versions of the ROG Ally X may come bundled with additional accessories such as:

Carrying Case:

A protective case to safeguard your device during travel.

Screen Protector:

An anti-scratch protector for keeping the display in pristine condition.

Docking Station:

For users who want to connect the Ally X to external monitors, eGPUs, or other peripherals.

The ASUS ROG Ally X is more than just a gaming console; it's a portable powerhouse that offers flexibility, high performance, and customization. Whether you're playing the latest AAA games, using it as a productivity tool, or running emulators for retro gaming, the Ally X provides an unparalleled experience in handheld gaming.

Chapter 1.

Getting Started

When you first receive your ASUS ROG Ally X, unboxing it will give you the first glimpse of this cutting-edge handheld gaming device. As you remove the device from its sleek packaging, you'll notice the attention to detail ASUS has given to both the console and its packaging. The device itself is compact but packs immense power, and every element of its design reflects its gaming pedigree.

Opening the box, you'll be greeted with the ROG Ally X sitting front and center, protected by foam inserts to ensure safe shipping. The packaging is designed to make the unboxing experience seamless, with compartments holding the power adapter, USB-C charging cable, and the Quick Start Guide easily accessible.

Once you remove the device, the feel of the ROG Ally X in your hands is immediately striking. The weight distribution is balanced, and its ergonomically contoured design ensures that it fits comfortably in your hands, even during extended gaming sessions. The matte finish gives the console a premium look, with the RGB lighting zones adding a modern, gamer-centric aesthetic.

The unboxing process is a chance to familiarize yourself with the device, inspect its build quality, and appreciate the overall design before diving into the performance features.

Overview of the Device:

The ROG Ally X is a powerful, all-in-one handheld gaming console designed to bring the PC gaming experience to a portable format. Below is an overview of the essential components and design elements of the device:

Dimensions:

The device is compact, with dimensions that strike a balance between portability and ease of use.

Display:

The 7-inch 1080p display supports a 120Hz refresh rate for smooth gameplay. It offers vibrant colors and crisp visuals, though it's not OLED.

Material:

The casing is made from durable, lightweight materials, making it sturdy without being too heavy for handheld gaming.

Controls:

The layout is designed for optimal ergonomics, featuring offset analog sticks, large ABXY buttons, and triggers for easy access during gameplay.

Ports and Connectivity:

Equipped with dual USB-C ports, a microSD slot, and a 3.5mm headphone jack, the ROG Ally X ensures that you have all the necessary connections for peripherals and accessories.

Buttons and Ports Layout:

To get the most out of your ROG Ally X, understanding the layout of its buttons and ports is crucial. Here's a breakdown of all the physical controls and connections on the device.

ABXY Buttons:

The ABXY buttons on the ROG Ally X are large, tactile, and positioned for easy access. They are similar in style and layout to the buttons on Xbox controllers, with a slight convex shape for comfortable pressing during intense gaming sessions. These buttons are responsive, making them ideal for both action-heavy games and titles requiring precise inputs.

Position:

Located on the right-hand side of the device, aligned in the traditional Xbox layout.

Functionality:

Used primarily for in-game actions, such as jumping, shooting, or interacting with objects.

Analog Sticks:

The analog sticks on the ROG Ally X are a highlight for many gamers, offering precision control with a comfortable feel. The concave design ensures your thumbs rest naturally on them, preventing slippage during fast-paced gameplay.

Design:

Offset in the style of an Xbox controller, the left analog stick is slightly higher than the right one.

Functionality:

Used for character movement, camera control, and navigating through in-game menus. They are durable and built for long-term use, supporting millions of input cycles.

D-Pad:

The D-pad on the ROG Ally X is a rounded, segmented design, differing from the more traditional cross-style D-pads seen on other controllers. This allows for smoother directional inputs and is ideal for fighting games, platformers, and retro titles.

Position:

Located beneath the left analog stick.

Functionality:

Primarily used for navigating menus, executing quick directional movements, or performing special commands in certain game genres.

Triggers and Bumpers:

The triggers and bumpers on the ROG Ally X are placed on the top of the device, offering tactile feedback and a solid response time. The improved design of the triggers provides more surface area and a better grip, enhancing your control in fast-action games.

Position:

Triggers (LT and RT) are located at the top rear corners, with bumpers (LB and RB) directly above them.

Functionality:

Triggers are typically used for acceleration, shooting, or aiming in games, while bumpers are often mapped to secondary actions like item selection or quick commands.

USB-C Ports:

The ROG Ally X is equipped with two USB-C ports, one of which supports USB4 for faster data transfer and eGPU connectivity. This allows for versatile charging options and the ability to connect various peripherals.

Position:

One port is located on the top of the device, with the second on the bottom or side, depending on the orientation.

Functionality:

Used for charging, connecting to external displays, or attaching accessories such as eGPUs or external storage.

MicroSD Slot:

The microSD slot on the ROG Ally X allows for easy expansion of storage beyond the internal SSD. This slot has been repositioned from the original Ally model to prevent overheating, ensuring that your microSD cards remain safe during extended gaming sessions.

Position:

Located on the side or bottom of the device.

Functionality:

Supports microSD cards for additional game storage or media expansion.

Headphone Jack:

The 3.5mm headphone jack is a classic feature on the ROG Ally X, catering to users who prefer wired audio solutions for low-latency sound. It allows for private, high-quality audio experiences without the need for wireless headphones.

Position:

Positioned on the top of the device for easy access.

Functionality:

Connects wired headphones or headsets for immersive audio.

Power and Volume Buttons:

The power and volume buttons are conveniently placed for easy access without interrupting gameplay. The power button doubles as a sleep/wake button, while the volume buttons allow you to adjust sound levels on the fly.

Position:

Located along the top of the device.

Functionality:

Power button controls device on/off and sleep mode. Volume buttons adjust system volume during gameplay.

Customizable RGB Lighting Zones:

The ROG Ally X features several RGB lighting zones that can be customized to reflect your personal style. You can change the colors and effects via the Armory Crate software, allowing for full control over how your device looks. The RGB lights are not just for aesthetics—they also serve as visual indicators for notifications or performance modes.

Position:

Located on the sides of the device, buttons, and around the analog sticks.

Functionality:

Adds a personal touch and visual feedback for specific events, such as power modes or charging status.

Charging and Battery Management:

The ASUS ROG Ally X comes with a 65W USB-C charger, designed for fast charging to minimize downtime between gaming sessions. Here's how you can effectively manage charging and battery life:

Charging the ROG Ally X:

To charge your device:

1. Connect the included USB-C charger to the USB-C charging port.

2. Plug the adapter into a power outlet.

3. The RGB lighting on the device will indicate charging status. Typically, the lights will pulse or change color when charging.

4. Full charging time can take approximately 2 hours from 0% to 100%.

Battery Life Tips:

Maximizing battery life is important for extended play sessions. Here are some tips:

1. Lower Screen Brightness:

Reducing the brightness can significantly improve battery longevity.

2. Use Lower Power Profiles:

Running games on lower settings or lower wattage modes (e.g., 13W mode) can extend battery life.

3. Disable Unnecessary Features:

Turn off Wi-Fi, Bluetooth, or RGB lighting when not needed.

4. Adjust In-Game Settings:

Lowering graphical settings or resolution can reduce power consumption, allowing for longer playtimes.

5. Close Background Apps:

Ensure that no unnecessary apps are running in the background to conserve power.

Power Profiles (13W, 17W, 25W Modes):

The ROG Ally X offers multiple power profiles to balance performance and battery life. These profiles allow you to customize the power output depending on the game's demands and your location (e.g., plugged in vs. on-the-go):

1. 13W Mode:

Ideal for indie games or less demanding titles.

Offers the longest battery life, with a focus on preserving power.

2. 17W Mode:

Balances performance and battery life, suitable for most games.

A middle-ground mode that provides a good mix of performance without draining the battery too quickly.

3. 25W Mode:

Maximizes performance for AAA titles and graphically demanding games.

Provides the best in-game experience, but battery life will be reduced.

Switching between these modes can be done through the Armory Crate software or via system settings, giving you the flexibility to adjust power consumption based on your needs.

Chapter 2.

Setting Up Your ROG Ally X

The ASUS ROG Ally X is designed to deliver a premium handheld gaming experience right out of the box. To ensure optimal performance and a smooth gaming experience, proper setup is crucial. This guide will walk you through the essential steps for getting your ROG Ally X ready for action, from initial configuration to installing the latest firmware and software updates.

Initial Setup and Configuration:

Upon turning on your ROG Ally X for the first time, you'll be guided through a series of steps to configure the device for your personal use. Here's a detailed guide on what to expect:

1. Power On:

Press the power button located on the top of the device. The ROG Ally X will boot up, and you'll be greeted with the ASUS splash screen followed by the Windows 11 setup wizard.

2. Language and Region Settings:

Choose your preferred language, region, and keyboard layout. These settings determine the default language of the system and regional preferences like date and time formatting.

3. Date and Time:

Set the correct time zone, date, and time. This is important for maintaining synchronization with online services and ensuring your device's clock is accurate.

4. Wi-Fi Connection:

Connect to a secure Wi-Fi network. You'll need an internet connection for account setup, Windows installation, and downloading updates. Enter the password for your Wi-Fi network, and the system will connect automatically.

5. Terms of Service:

Read and accept the ASUS terms and conditions as well as the Windows license agreement. These are necessary to proceed with the setup.

6. Microsoft Account Sign-In:

If you have a Microsoft account, sign in to sync your settings, apps, and files across devices. If you don't have an account, you can create one during this step, or alternatively, proceed with a local account if you prefer not to link your device to a Microsoft account.

7. OneDrive Setup:

During the setup, you'll be prompted to configure OneDrive, Microsoft's cloud storage service. You can choose to back up your files to OneDrive to keep them secure and accessible across devices, or skip this step if you don't want to use cloud storage.

8. Security Options:

You'll be given the option to set up Windows Hello, which includes biometric options like facial recognition (if available) or a PIN for quick and secure sign-in. Setting up a PIN is recommended for quicker access to your device.

9. Device Customization:

After completing these basic configurations, you'll be asked to choose your preferences for things like privacy settings, diagnostics, and data sharing. These settings can affect how much information is shared with Microsoft, ASUS, and third-party apps.

Once these steps are completed, Windows 11 will finalize the initial setup and take you to the desktop, where you can start exploring your ROG Ally X.

Connecting to Wi-Fi and Microsoft Account Setup:

For the best experience, especially if you plan on utilizing cloud gaming services, downloading new games, or syncing settings, it's important to establish a reliable Wi-Fi connection during the initial setup.

1. Wi-Fi Setup:

Navigate to Settings > Network & Internet and ensure Wi-Fi is enabled. Select your preferred network from the list of available options and enter the password. Make sure you are connected to a stable and fast Wi-Fi network, preferably on the 5GHz band for optimal gaming and downloading speeds.

2. Microsoft Account Setup:

Signing into your Microsoft account allows for synchronization of your OneDrive, Microsoft Store purchases, and other services. If you already have an account, you can enter your credentials. If you don't, you'll have the option to create one. This step is essential if you plan to access the Xbox Game Pass service, use Microsoft Office, or sync with other Windows devices.

Windows 11 Installation and Settings Overview:

The ROG Ally X runs on Windows 11, which means you have access to a full-fledged operating system, allowing for extensive customization and the ability to run desktop applications. Once you've completed the initial setup, it's important to familiarize yourself with the core Windows 11 features and settings:

1. Start Menu and Taskbar:

The Start Menu is centered on the screen by default, giving you quick access to apps, settings, and recently used documents. The Taskbar at the bottom shows running applications and system notifications.

2. File Explorer:

Familiarize yourself with the File Explorer, where you can manage files, install games, and organize your storage. Since the ROG Ally X supports expandable storage via a microSD card, you may want to set up separate folders for games, apps, and media to keep things organized.

3. Windows Settings:

Access Windows Settings by pressing Windows + I. Here, you can configure essential features like display resolution, audio settings, and network preferences. Take some time to explore the different categories and personalize your device based on your gaming needs and system requirements.

4. Gaming Settings:

Windows 11 includes a dedicated Gaming section where you can enable features like Game Mode (which optimizes system performance for gaming), configure Xbox Game Bar, and adjust graphics settings for a smoother gaming experience.

5. Windows Updates:

Ensure your device is up to date by going to Settings > Windows Update. Keeping Windows and your drivers up to date ensures that your ROG Ally X runs smoothly, improves performance, and enhances security.

Updating Firmware and Drivers:

Keeping your ROG Ally X up to date with the latest firmware and drivers is critical for optimal performance and stability. ASUS regularly releases updates that address system bugs, improve compatibility, and enhance gaming features.

1. Check for Updates:

Navigate to Settings > Windows Update to check for the latest updates. Windows will automatically search for updates, including essential firmware and driver patches. Make sure you are connected to the internet before initiating this step.

2. ASUS Support:

For manual updates, visit the ASUS support page and search for your device model (ROG Ally X). Here, you can find firmware updates, driver downloads, and patch notes for recent updates.

3. Install Drivers:

Drivers for components like the AMD Ryzen Z1 Extreme processor, display, Wi-Fi, and USB-C ports are vital for maintaining smooth performance. Make sure to download and install the latest versions if they aren't automatically updated through Windows Update.

4. BIOS/Firmware Updates:

Periodically, ASUS releases BIOS or firmware updates to improve system stability and introduce new features. BIOS updates should be handled carefully, so it's best to follow ASUS's official guide for safe installation.

Installing ASUS Armoury Crate Software:

One of the key software components for managing your ROG Ally X is ASUS Armoury Crate. This powerful tool centralizes all gaming-related settings, from performance profiles to RGB lighting controls.

1. Download and Install:

Armoury Crate may come pre-installed, but if not, you can download it from the Microsoft Store or directly from the ASUS website. Follow the installation prompts to install the software on your device.

2. Configuring Armoury Crate:

Once installed, launch the Armoury Crate app. This tool lets you:

Monitor system performance:

Track CPU, GPU, and RAM usage in real time.

Adjust power profiles:

Switch between the 13W, 17W, and 25W power modes to balance performance and battery life.

Manage RGB lighting:

Customize the RGB lighting zones with different effects and colors to match your gaming setup.

Game Library:

Organize your game library and launch games directly from Armoury Crate.

3. Creating Performance Profiles:

You can create custom performance profiles for specific games or applications. For example, you may want to set higher power limits for AAA games and lower power settings for less demanding titles.

4. Firmware Updates via Armoury Crate:

Armoury Crate also provides a dedicated section for checking and installing ASUS firmware updates. This ensures that your device is always running the latest system firmware, keeping it optimized for gaming.

By setting up Armoury Crate, you can fine-tune the performance of your ROG Ally X, making sure you get the best possible experience based on your gaming preferences.

Properly setting up your ASUS ROG Ally X ensures you're ready for the most seamless, immersive gaming experience available on a portable handheld device. With Windows 11, the latest firmware, and customizable features through Armoury Crate, you'll have a highly adaptable gaming system in the palm of your hand.

Chapter 3.

Customizing the ROG Ally X

The ASUS ROG Ally X is designed with personalization and customization in mind, allowing gamers to fine-tune their experience for both aesthetics and performance. From customizable RGB lighting to button remapping and display adjustments, the Ally X offers a range of options to make your device uniquely yours. This chapter will guide you through how to personalize key features like lighting, buttons, display settings, and audio configurations to create an optimized gaming setup that fits your preferences.

RGB Lighting Customization:

One of the signature features of the ROG Ally X is its vibrant and customizable RGB lighting. The RGB zones on the device can be modified to reflect your style, provide visual feedback during gameplay, or sync with other ROG devices.

1. Accessing RGB Settings in Armoury Crate:

Open the Armoury Crate software, which is the central hub for controlling all customization features, including RGB lighting.

Navigate to the Device or Lighting tab, where you'll find the settings for RGB zones. The ROG Ally X has multiple lighting zones, such as around the analog sticks and along the edges of the device.

2. Lighting Effects:

Armoury Crate offers a variety of pre-configured lighting effects that can be applied to the device, such as:

Static:

A single, constant color of your choice.

Breathing:

Pulsing on and off in your chosen color(s).

Rainbow:

A rotating spectrum of colors across all zones.

Strobe:

Flashing light patterns for a more dramatic effect.

Reactive:

Lights that respond to in-game actions or sound cues.

Music Sync:

Lighting that changes rhythmically with the music you're playing through the system.

3. Customizing Colors:

Choose your desired colors using the color wheel or by inputting specific RGB values. Armoury Crate allows for precise color control across different zones, meaning you can have one zone with a static red while another features a breathing blue effect.

For gamers who own other ASUS Aura Sync devices (keyboards, mice, etc.), the RGB lighting on the ROG Ally X can be synchronized with those peripherals for a cohesive lighting setup.

4. Creating Lighting Profiles:

You can create and save different lighting profiles for various uses or games. For example, you might want a more subdued lighting profile for casual gaming and a vibrant, reactive profile for competitive play.

5. Setting Up Game-Specific Lighting:

Armoury Crate also lets you associate specific RGB profiles with individual games. When you launch a game, the device will automatically switch to the lighting profile you've assigned to it.

Button Remapping and Profiles:

The ROG Ally X offers extensive customization options for its physical controls, including button remapping, so you can tailor the control scheme to your playstyle or the specific needs of different games.

1. Button Remapping:

Open the Armoury Crate software and navigate to the Control Settings tab.

You'll be able to remap the ABXY buttons, D-pad, triggers, and bumpers. For instance, if a certain game feels more intuitive with the X button mapped to a different action, you can easily change this through the interface.

The remapping feature is particularly useful for games that don't natively support custom control schemes or for players who prefer an alternate button layout.

2. Creating Custom Profiles:

Profiles allow you to save specific button configurations for different games or applications. For example, you can create a custom profile for a first-person shooter with rapid trigger response and another for a platformer with specific D-pad settings.

Armoury Crate also allows you to assign profiles to specific games, ensuring that the device automatically switches to the correct configuration when you launch a particular title.

3. Adjusting Analog Stick Sensitivity:

Through the Armoury Crate, you can adjust the sensitivity of the analog sticks. This feature is useful for both precision aiming in shooters or fast movements in action games. You can fine-tune the dead zones and response curves to suit your style of play.

4. Trigger and Bumper Customization:

The triggers and bumpers can also be customized for travel distance and pressure sensitivity, particularly useful in racing games or shooters where trigger control affects acceleration or firing mechanics.

Adjusting Display Settings (Resolution, Refresh Rate)

The ROG Ally X comes with a 7-inch 1080p 120Hz VRR (Variable Refresh Rate) display, offering high-quality visuals for handheld gaming. Customizing your display settings can help optimize the balance between graphical fidelity and performance.

1. Resolution:

By default, the device runs at 1080p, which delivers sharp, detailed visuals. However, for less demanding games or to conserve battery life, you may choose to lower the resolution.

To adjust the resolution, navigate to Settings > System > Display in Windows 11. Here, you can lower the resolution to 720p or other supported resolutions depending on your preference.

2. Refresh Rate:

The ROG Ally X supports a refresh rate of up to 120Hz, providing smoother gameplay and more fluid motion, particularly beneficial in fast-paced action games or shooters.

To change the refresh rate, go to Settings > System > Display > Advanced Display Settings. Here, you can toggle between different refresh rates like 60Hz, 90Hz, and 120Hz, depending on your gaming needs and battery considerations. A lower refresh rate can help extend battery life, while higher rates provide smoother visuals.

3. Brightness and Contrast:

Adjust the screen brightness through Settings > System > Display. For better visibility outdoors or in brightly lit environments, increase the brightness, while dimming it can conserve power during extended gaming sessions.

4. Enabling Night Mode:

Windows 11 includes a Night Light feature, which reduces blue light emission and makes the display easier on your eyes during long gaming sessions, especially at night. To enable this, go to Settings > System > Display > Night Light.

5. Calibrating Color:

You can further refine your display's color balance and saturation through the Windows Color Calibration tool found in Display Settings. This is useful for adjusting the screen to match your personal color preferences or to optimize visuals for specific games.

Audio Settings and Headphone Configuration:

Great sound is an essential part of the gaming experience, and the ROG Ally X is equipped with several ways to customize and enhance audio quality.

1. Internal Speakers:

The ROG Ally X comes with built-in stereo speakers, providing clear and immersive sound for gaming. You can adjust the volume via the volume rocker on the device or through Windows Settings > System > Sound.

For enhanced sound quality, enable Spatial Sound (Windows Sonic) under the Sound Settings. This feature provides a 3D audio effect that enhances immersion in games that support positional audio.

2. Headphone Jack:

For those who prefer gaming with headphones, the ROG Ally X features a 3.5mm headphone jack on top of the device. You can plug in any standard headphones for better audio isolation and richer sound. The jack is optimized for both stereo and surround sound headphones.

3. Bluetooth Headphones:

The ROG Ally X also supports Bluetooth 5.2, allowing you to pair wireless headphones for cable-free audio. To connect, go to Settings > Bluetooth & Devices, turn on Bluetooth, and pair your Bluetooth headphones.

For the best gaming experience, ensure your Bluetooth headphones support low-latency modes, which can help reduce audio lag during gameplay.

4. Customizing Audio Settings in Armoury Crate:

Through Armoury Crate, you can further adjust audio profiles. These profiles allow you to enhance specific frequencies (bass, treble, mids) depending on the type of game or media you are using. For instance, you may want more bass during action games and clearer treble for dialogue-heavy RPGs.

5. Microphone Settings:

If you use a headset with a microphone for multiplayer gaming or voice chat, you can customize the microphone sensitivity and enable noise reduction in Windows Sound Settings.

Armoury Crate offers additional noise cancellation options that improve the clarity of your voice during online gaming sessions.

Conclusion:

Customizing the ROG Ally X allows you to create a highly personalized gaming experience. Whether you're optimizing visuals for maximum performance, adjusting audio for immersive sound, or customizing button layouts for specific games, the flexibility of the Ally X ensures that you're always in control. By taking advantage of Armoury Crate's customization features and Windows 11 settings, you can fine-tune every aspect of your device to suit your style and preferences.

Chapter 4.

Navigating Windows 11 on ROG Ally X

The ASUS ROG Ally X offers a unique fusion of PC gaming and handheld portability by running Windows 11, a full-fledged desktop operating system, on a gaming handheld. This gives users the power of a desktop PC while offering flexibility to switch between gaming-focused handheld mode and full desktop functionality. Navigating Windows 11 on a compact device like the ROG Ally X comes with its own set of challenges and optimizations to ensure a smooth experience whether you're gaming, streaming, or working.

Using Windows 11 on a Handheld Console:

Running Windows 11 on the ROG Ally X means having access to a complete operating system typically found on desktops and laptops, making it ideal for gamers who need flexibility beyond just gaming. Whether you're using it for work, entertainment, or high-performance gaming, the transition between these functions is seamless, thanks to the robust nature of the OS.

1. Touchscreen Interface:

The 7-inch 1080p touchscreen of the ROG Ally X allows you to interact with Windows 11 using touch gestures, such as swiping, pinching, and tapping, much like on a smartphone or tablet.

Windows 11 has been optimized for touch devices, so you'll find it easy to navigate menus, open apps, and manage settings. Familiar gestures like swiping from the right edge to bring up the Action Center or swiping from the left to open the Start Menu are highly intuitive.

2. Start Menu and Taskbar:

The Start Menu is where you'll find your installed apps, system settings, and recently used files. Tapping the Windows icon on the bottom center of the screen will bring up the Start

Menu, where you can search for apps or documents using the on-screen keyboard.

The Taskbar at the bottom offers quick access to essential apps and system functions like volume control, network settings, and battery management. You can customize the Taskbar to add shortcuts to your most-used apps or games.

3. Window Management:

Windows 11 on the ROG Ally X supports Snap Layouts, a feature that allows you to organize multiple windows on the screen. This is especially useful when multitasking, like playing a game while also streaming, or when you need to monitor system stats while gaming. You can quickly snap windows to the side of the screen by dragging them to the edges.

4. On-Screen Keyboard:

While the device comes with physical ABXY buttons, triggers, and analog sticks for gaming, you'll likely use the on-screen keyboard for text input when navigating Windows 11. The keyboard can be activated by tapping on text fields and can be customized in size and layout for comfortable typing.

Switching Between Handheld Mode and Desktop Mode:

The ROG Ally X is designed to function as both a handheld gaming device and a full Windows PC. To cater to these two distinct use cases, you can easily switch between Handheld Mode and Desktop Mode.

1. Handheld Mode:

Handheld Mode is optimized for gaming, giving you access to key gaming features like quick access to games, performance monitoring, and control settings, while minimizing desktop elements that might clutter the screen.

In Handheld Mode, the device prioritizes gaming performance. The desktop is simplified, and key shortcuts for launching games via platforms like Steam, Xbox Game Pass, or the Epic Games Store are prominent.

To switch to Handheld Mode, you can use the Armoury Crate SE interface, a gaming hub that allows for quick access to games, system performance settings, and battery profiles. This mode emphasizes ease of navigation using physical buttons and joystick controls rather than relying on touch or mouse input.

2. Desktop Mode:

When you want to use the ROG Ally X like a traditional PC, Desktop Mode allows full access to Windows 11's suite of productivity tools. This is ideal for tasks like video editing, writing, or browsing the web, where you need the power of a full desktop operating system.

In Desktop Mode, the entire Windows 11 interface is available, including the full Start Menu, Taskbar, and window management features. This mode is best suited when you've connected an external keyboard and mouse for productivity tasks.

Switching between Handheld and Desktop Modes is as simple as pressing a button in the Armoury Crate SE, or you can automate this process when connecting an external monitor or docking station.

3. Optimizing Performance:

Windows 11's Power Modes can be adjusted based on whether you're in Handheld or Desktop Mode. For example, while in Handheld Mode, you might choose to optimize battery life, whereas in Desktop Mode, you can increase performance for more demanding tasks.

Desktop Shortcuts for Quick Access:

To streamline your experience in Desktop Mode, creating shortcuts for quick access to frequently used apps, settings, and games is crucial. The ROG Ally X's smaller screen size makes efficient navigation essential.

1. Pinning Apps to the Taskbar:

You can pin your favorite apps and games to the Taskbar for easy access. Right-click on any app in the Start Menu or File Explorer and choose Pin to Taskbar.

Common shortcuts for the Taskbar might include Steam, Xbox Game Pass, ASUS Armoury Crate, and your most-used productivity tools like Microsoft Edge or File Explorer.

2. Creating Desktop Shortcuts:

For quick access to games or applications, create desktop shortcuts by right-clicking on an app and selecting Create Shortcut. You can organize these shortcuts into folders or group them into categories to keep the desktop uncluttered.

Consider grouping game launchers (like Epic Games, GOG Galaxy, and Steam) in a single folder for easy access in both Handheld and Desktop Modes.

3. Setting Up Hotkeys for Game Launch:

In Armoury Crate, you can assign custom hotkeys to launch specific games or applications quickly. For instance, you might set a combination of L1 + B to launch a specific game or media app without navigating through multiple menus.

Setting Up External Monitors and eGPU:

The ROG Ally X supports external displays and can be connected to an eGPU (External Graphics Processing Unit) to dramatically boost its graphical performance when docked. This transforms the Ally X into a high-powered gaming PC for competitive play or content creation.

1. Connecting to External Monitors:

The ROG Ally X features USB-C ports with DisplayPort support, which can be used to connect to external monitors or TVs. To do this, you'll need a USB-C to HDMI or USB-C to DisplayPort adapter, depending on the monitor's input.

Once connected, the external monitor will either mirror the display of the ROG Ally X or extend it, depending on your settings in Display Settings. You can adjust the resolution and refresh rate of the external display for optimal performance, ensuring smooth gameplay at higher resolutions like 1440p or 4K.

You can also choose to turn off the ROG Ally X's display and use only the external monitor for better performance.

2. Dual Monitor Setup:

In Desktop Mode, you can use the Dual Monitor feature, treating the ROG Ally X's screen as a secondary monitor. This is particularly useful if you want to use the main display for gaming while using the Ally X's screen for multitasking, such as monitoring game performance or streaming software.

To configure multiple displays, go to Settings > System > Display and choose how you want the monitors arranged (Extend, Duplicate, or Second Screen Only).

3. Using an eGPU (External Graphics Processing Unit):

The ROG Ally X is compatible with eGPUs via its USB-C port, allowing you to connect a high-performance external graphics card to enhance your gaming experience. This setup is ideal if you want to play graphically demanding games at higher resolutions and frame rates while docked.

Once connected to an eGPU, the Ally X can automatically switch to use the external GPU's processing power for tasks, offloading the graphical load from the internal integrated graphics. This can provide a significant performance boost, allowing for smoother gameplay and higher graphical settings.

When using an eGPU, you can also benefit from more VRAM (Video RAM), enabling better handling of 4K gaming, ray tracing, or VR applications.

4. Optimizing for Docked Mode:

When using external monitors or eGPUs, it's recommended to switch to the higher power profiles available in the Armoury Crate (such as 25W or above), ensuring the device can take full advantage of its connected peripherals.

In Docked Mode, you can configure different performance profiles to automatically enable higher refresh rates, better resolution, and more system resources for multitasking.

Conclusion:

Navigating Windows 11 on the ROG Ally X is a powerful experience that provides flexibility for both gaming and productivity. Whether you're playing games in Handheld Mode, working in Desktop Mode, or connected to an external monitor with an eGPU, the Ally X is designed to handle it all. By leveraging the customizable desktop shortcuts, seamless switching between modes,

Chapter 5.

Gaming on the ROG Ally X

The ROG Ally X is a versatile handheld gaming device that brings the full power of a Windows 11 PC to your fingertips. This flexibility allows users to run games from various digital storefronts such as Steam, Epic Games Store, GOG, and Xbox Game Pass for PC. In this chapter, we'll dive into how to install and run games on the ROG Ally X, explore its performance modes for optimized gaming, discuss ways to adjust in-game settings, customize your experience using Armoury Crate, manage game libraries, and expand your storage options, including upgrading the internal SSD.

Installing and Running Games (Steam, Epic, GOG, etc.):

With the ROG Ally X running on Windows 11, you can install and play games from virtually any platform, turning the device into an all-in-one gaming machine.

1. Steam:

Steam is one of the largest and most popular platforms for PC gaming, offering a vast library of AAA and indie titles. Installing Steam on the ROG Ally X is as easy as downloading the client from the official website. Once installed, you can access your entire library and install games directly onto the internal storage or external storage solutions like a MicroSD card or external SSD. Steam's Big Picture Mode is perfect for the Ally X, optimizing the interface for controller use and making navigation more intuitive.

2. Epic Games Store:

The Epic Games Store offers its own library of exclusive titles and frequent free game giveaways. Downloading and installing the Epic client works similarly to Steam. Though it doesn't have a controller-optimized interface like Big Picture Mode, the ROG Ally X's touchscreen and built-in controls still allow for smooth navigation. Games like Fortnite, Rocket League, and Borderlands 3 run well on the device, especially when performance modes are adjusted to match the game's requirements.

3. GOG Galaxy:

For gamers who prefer DRM-free titles, GOG Galaxy provides a seamless experience on the ROG Ally X. The platform is ideal for playing both retro classics and modern games. Many of GOG's older titles, such as Baldur's Gate and Planescape: Torment, run effortlessly on the device, while more graphically demanding games like The Witcher 3 can benefit from tweaking performance settings to find the right balance between visual fidelity and battery life.

4. Xbox Game Pass for PC:

Xbox Game Pass for PC provides access to hundreds of games for a monthly subscription fee. Once you've installed the Xbox app, you can quickly access and install games from the Game Pass library. The app also integrates with Xbox Cloud Gaming, allowing you to stream games without using much storage. Game Pass is a great option for gamers who want to try out a wide range of games without making individual purchases.

5. Emulation:

The ROG Ally X's hardware is powerful enough to run a variety of emulators, making it a great device for retro gaming. Programs like RetroArch, PCSX2, and Dolphin allow you to emulate games from older systems like the NES, PlayStation 2, and GameCube. The device's ability to handle high-performance emulation means you can play your favorite classics on the go with enhanced performance and smoother visuals.

Performance Modes for Optimized Gaming:

The ROG Ally X provides multiple performance modes that allow you to optimize your gaming experience based on the demands of the game and your power source. These performance modes can be accessed through Armoury Crate SE, ASUS's proprietary software designed for system management.

1. 13W Eco Mode:

Eco Mode is ideal for conserving battery life when you're playing less demanding games or retro titles. By capping power consumption at 13 watts, the ROG Ally X runs cooler and quieter, extending battery life while still delivering solid performance for games like Celeste, Stardew Valley, or emulated classics.

2. 17W Balanced Mode:

Balanced Mode strikes a compromise between performance and power efficiency. It's suitable for most modern games, providing enough power to maintain smooth frame rates while preserving battery life. Titles like Resident Evil Village or Assassin's Creed Valhalla run well in this mode, especially when paired with medium graphical settings.

3. 25W Performance Mode:

For graphically intensive games, Performance Mode unlocks the full potential of the ROG Ally X's hardware. Drawing 25 watts of power, this mode is best used when the device is plugged in. It's ideal for demanding AAA titles such as Cyberpunk 2077 or Red Dead Redemption 2, where you need maximum performance to maintain high frame rates and graphical fidelity.

Adjusting In-Game Settings for Better Performance:

Even with performance modes, some games may require fine-tuning to achieve the best gaming experience. Here are key settings you can adjust to optimize performance:

1. Resolution:

The Ally X features a 1080p display, but lowering the resolution to 720p can improve performance significantly without sacrificing much visual quality. This is particularly useful for more graphically demanding games, as it can boost frame rates and extend battery life during long gaming sessions.

2. Graphics Quality:

In most games, reducing settings such as texture quality, shadows, and anti-aliasing can dramatically improve performance. Disabling features like motion blur or lowering post-processing effects like bloom can also give you smoother gameplay without a significant loss in visual appeal.

3. Frame Rate Limits:

Capping your frame rate at 30 or 60 FPS can help stabilize performance, particularly when playing on battery power.

Many games allow you to manually limit frame rates, ensuring smoother gameplay while reducing the power drain.

4. V-Sync and G-Sync:

Enabling or disabling V-Sync can help reduce screen tearing, though it may slightly impact performance. If your game stutters or tears frequently, experimenting with V-Sync settings can help stabilize visuals.

Using Armoury Crate for Game Customization:

Armoury Crate is the central hub for managing performance settings, system monitoring, and custom profiles on the ROG Ally X. It's a powerful tool that lets you fine-tune the device to match your specific gaming needs.

1. Custom Profiles:

Armoury Crate allows you to create custom profiles for each game, specifying performance modes, fan settings, and control mappings. This is especially useful if you switch between games with different performance needs, as it saves you from manually adjusting settings each time.

2. System Monitoring:

Armoury Crate provides real-time monitoring of CPU and GPU usage, temperature, and battery life. This feature is handy for ensuring your system isn't overheating or running too hot during extended gaming sessions, helping you maintain optimal performance.

Managing Game Libraries and External Storage:

With modern games taking up tens or even hundreds of gigabytes, storage management is crucial on the ROG Ally X. Fortunately, the device offers multiple options for expanding and managing your game library.

1. Using the MicroSD Slot:

The ROG Ally X comes with a MicroSD card slot, allowing you to easily expand storage with a high-speed UHS-I or UHS-II MicroSD card. Cards up to 1TB are supported, making them a great option for storing games, particularly larger AAA titles that might not fit on the internal SSD.

2. External Storage Solutions:

You can also connect an external SSD or HDD to the Ally X via its USB-C port. This provides additional storage for games that you don't want to keep on the internal drive. External SSDs are ideal for fast load times and transferring large files between devices.

Expanding Internal Storage (SSD Upgrade Guide)

If you find that external storage options are not enough, you can upgrade the ROG Ally X's internal SSD. The device uses a M.2 2230 SSD, which can be replaced to expand your internal storage up to 2TB.

1. Choosing an SSD:

To upgrade, you'll need a compatible M.2 2230 SSD. Brands like Western Digital and Samsung offer reliable options.

Ensure the SSD you choose fits the 2230 form factor and offers enough capacity for your needs.

2. Installing the SSD:

Opening the ROG Ally X requires some care, but ASUS provides detailed guides on safely removing the back panel. Once inside, locate the existing SSD, remove it, and replace it with the new one. After installation, you may need to reinstall Windows or clone your existing drive.

By following these steps, you can significantly expand the Ally X's storage, making room for more games and applications without relying on external drives.

Chapter 6.

Emulation on the ROG Ally X

One of the most exciting features of the ASUS ROG Ally X is its versatility as a retro gaming powerhouse. Emulation allows you to relive classic titles from a wide range of consoles, all on a single device. With its robust hardware, Windows 11 OS, and built-in controllers, the Ally X is ideal for running emulators for systems like the NES, SNES, PlayStation 2, GameCube, and even more demanding platforms such as the Nintendo Switch and PlayStation 3. This chapter covers the process of installing emulators, running retro games, and configuring the best settings for each platform to ensure optimal performance.

Installing Emulators:

Before you can start playing retro games on your ROG Ally X, you'll need to install emulators. Emulators are software programs that mimic the hardware of older gaming systems, allowing you to run classic games (also known as ROMs). There are different emulators for various consoles, and some are more optimized for performance than others.

1. RetroArch:

RetroArch is one of the most popular and versatile emulation platforms available. It supports a wide range of systems, from early consoles like the Atari 2600 to more recent platforms like the PlayStation Portable (PSP). RetroArch uses a modular design, allowing you to download and install separate "cores" for each console you want to emulate. To install RetroArch on the ROG Ally X:

Visit the RetroArch website and download the Windows version.

Install the software and launch it.

Once in the app, navigate to the "Online Updater" and select Core Updater to download the specific emulator cores for the systems you want to emulate.

After setting up your cores, you can begin loading your ROMs and configuring your controls.

2. Dolphin (GameCube/Wii Emulator)

For emulating GameCube and Wii games, Dolphin is the go-to emulator. It's highly optimized for both performance and graphical fidelity, making it a perfect choice for the ROG Ally X.

Download Dolphin from its official website.

After installation, you can configure settings like controller input, graphical enhancements, and game profiles. Dolphin is particularly well-suited to the Ally X, as many GameCube and Wii games can run at higher resolutions with improved textures.

Dolphin also supports using Ally's built-in controls for an authentic console experience.

3. PCSX2 (PlayStation 2 Emulator)

PCSX2 is a powerful emulator for the PlayStation 2, a system that still boasts one of the largest libraries of games. It's more demanding than older emulators, but the Ally X's hardware is more than capable of running most games at higher resolutions.

Download the PCSX2 emulator from its website.

Install the necessary BIOS files, which are essential for running PlayStation 2 games (you must dump your own BIOS from a PS2 system to use legally).

After setup, configure graphics settings to your desired resolution, and map the Ally X's controls for a native-feeling experience.

4. Cemu (Wii U Emulator)

Cemu is a great choice for running Wii U games, which allows you to play titles like The Legend of Zelda: Breath of the Wild on the ROG Ally X.

Download Cemu from its website and install it.

Configure your controls, resolution, and graphical settings.

Cemu supports several mods and enhancements that can improve visuals, making your gaming experience even better than on the original Wii U hardware.

5. RPCS3 (PlayStation 3 Emulator)

For PlayStation 3 games, RPCS3 is a powerful emulator that takes advantage of the Ally X's robust specs.

Download RPCS3 from the official site.

You'll need to dump the PS3 firmware and BIOS files from a real PlayStation 3.

RPCS3 allows you to customize graphics settings, scale resolution, and optimize performance based on your hardware. While more demanding games may require some tweaking, many titles run at high frame rates and resolution, providing a seamless experience.

6. Yuzu (Nintendo Switch Emulator)

If you want to play Nintendo Switch games, Yuzu is the most advanced emulator for this purpose.

Download Yuzu from its official website.

You'll need to dump the necessary keys and firmware from your Nintendo Switch console (this step is required for legal usage).

After setting up Yuzu, you can configure graphics settings to run games at higher resolutions and improve performance. Many games are playable with minimal tweaking.

Running Retro Games:

Once you've installed your emulators, you'll need to load your games. For legal reasons, it's important to use ROMs from your own physical copies of games. Dumping ROMs from your own cartridges or discs ensures that you're not violating copyright laws. Many emulators provide built-in tools or third-party applications that help with the dumping process.

To load a ROM:

1. Launch the emulator of your choice (e.g., RetroArch, Dolphin, PCSX2).

2. From the emulator's main interface, browse for the ROM or ISO file that corresponds to the game you want to play.

3. Configure your controls (if needed) and start the game.

For most older systems like the NES, SNES, or Sega Genesis, the Ally X can easily handle emulation with little to no performance adjustments. The games will run smoothly even at high resolutions, and the Ally X's built-in controls make it feel like you're playing on the original hardware.

However, for more demanding platforms like the PlayStation 2, GameCube, or Wii U, you may need to adjust performance settings to optimize gameplay. This can include lowering the resolution, disabling certain graphical enhancements, or capping the frame rate to ensure smooth performance without overtaxing the system.

Recommended Emulator Settings and Tools:

To get the most out of your emulation experience on the ROG Ally X, it's essential to configure each emulator to optimize both performance and visual quality. Here are some general settings and tools that work well across different emulators.

1. Resolution Scaling

Many emulators support resolution scaling, which allows you to run games at a higher resolution than the original hardware. This feature can make older games look much better on modern displays. For example, you can run GameCube or PlayStation 2 games at 1080p or even 4K on the ROG Ally X, significantly improving the image quality. However, resolution scaling can be demanding, so adjust it based on the game's performance.

2. Texture Filtering

Anisotropic filtering and bilinear/trilinear filtering can be enabled to improve the texture quality of older games. These settings smooth out pixelated textures and make them look cleaner on high-resolution screens. Most emulators include these options in the graphics settings menu.

3. Frame Rate Settings

Some games may run faster or slower depending on the emulation accuracy. Locking the frame rate at the console's native speed (e.g., 60fps for many newer systems, 30fps for older ones) ensures that the games don't run too quickly or with uneven pacing.

4. Shader Effects

Emulators like RetroArch offer shader effects that can mimic the look of older CRT monitors or add visual enhancements like scanlines and bloom effects. These shaders can improve the visual experience for retro games by recreating the nostalgic feel of playing on old TVs.

5. Save States

Save states allow you to save the game at any point, making it easier to pick up where you left off. This is especially useful for older games that don't have built-in save features. Each emulator has its own save state system, and RetroArch, for instance, lets you assign quick save/load buttons to streamline this process.

6. Input Mapping and Controller Customization

The ROG Ally X's built-in controllers are perfect for most emulated games, but each emulator lets you remap buttons based on personal preference or game requirements. For example, RetroArch lets you assign hotkeys for specific actions like fast-forwarding, quick saving, or swapping disks (for multi-disk games).

7. Third-Party Tools

Tools like EmulationStation or LaunchBox can help organize your game library and provide a polished interface for navigating and launching your ROMs. These frontends allow you to organize your games by console, genre, or release date, making it easier to access your favorite titles.

By following these recommendations, you'll get the best possible experience when running emulated games on the ROG Ally X. Whether you're reliving the golden age of 8-bit and 16-bit gaming or pushing the limits of more recent consoles, the Ally X's powerful hardware and flexible Windows platform make it a fantastic device for emulation.

Chapter 7.

Advanced Features

The ASUS ROG Ally X is not just a gaming handheld; it's a versatile and powerful machine capable of handling more advanced gaming and productivity tasks. This chapter delves into the most cutting-edge features available on the ROG Ally X, including setting up an external GPU (eGPU), exploring virtual reality compatibility, streaming games from your PC or other devices, and connecting additional controllers and peripherals via wireless or Bluetooth.

eGPU Setup and Usage:

While the ROG Ally X is a powerful gaming device on its own, it truly shines when paired with an eGPU (External Graphics Processing Unit) for even better graphical performance. Using an eGPU can transform the Ally X into a full-fledged gaming desktop capable of playing the most demanding AAA titles at higher settings, improving performance and frame rates.

1. Why Use an eGPU? Although the Ally X comes equipped with a robust internal GPU, it's not as powerful as some desktop-class GPUs available on the market. With an eGPU, you can take advantage of desktop-level performance, pushing 4K resolution, maxing out graphic settings, and enjoying ray tracing features that may be more limited in handheld mode. An eGPU allows you to seamlessly transition from handheld gaming to desktop-class gaming, offering greater flexibility.

2. Choosing an eGPU Enclosure To use an eGPU with the ROG Ally X, you'll need an eGPU enclosure, which houses the graphics card and connects it to your Ally X via a high-speed interface like Thunderbolt 4 or USB-C. Some popular eGPU enclosures include the Razer Core X and ASUS ROG XG Station Pro, which are compatible with a wide range of GPUs from NVIDIA and AMD.

3. Setting Up an eGPU

Step 1:

Install your desktop-class GPU into the eGPU enclosure. Follow the specific instructions for your chosen enclosure.

Step 2:

Connect the eGPU enclosure to the ROG Ally X via USB-C or Thunderbolt 4.

Step 3:

Power on the enclosure and ensure the ROG Ally X detects the external GPU.

Step 4:

Install or update the GPU drivers. Windows 11 should automatically detect the new hardware and prompt you to install the appropriate drivers.

Step 5:

Configure the settings for which games and applications should use the eGPU for performance.

Once set up, you can enjoy a significant boost in graphical performance, particularly for high-end AAA games, video editing, and other graphically intensive applications. The setup is ideal for those who want a dual-purpose device, using the Ally X for portable gaming but docking it with an eGPU for a desktop-class gaming experience.

4. Optimizing Performance with eGPU While the eGPU will provide additional power, optimizing game settings is essential to get the most out of it. For example, adjusting in-game settings to 4K, enabling ray tracing, or increasing the graphical detail will now be possible with more headroom, thanks to the eGPU's power.

Virtual Reality Compatibility (VR):

The ROG Ally X can also serve as an entry point into the world of Virtual Reality (VR) gaming. Although it's not a VR device on its own, the Ally X can connect to VR systems like the Oculus Quest 2 or Valve Index via PC VR solutions, allowing you to enjoy immersive gaming experiences.

1. VR Requirements To use VR with the ROG Ally X, the device must meet the minimum specifications required by VR headsets. The internal GPU of the Ally X can handle less

demanding VR experiences, but for more advanced games, you may need to use an eGPU or lower in-game settings to ensure smooth performance.

2. Setting Up VR on ROG Ally X

Step 1:

Install the required VR software, such as SteamVR for PC-based VR headsets or Oculus Link for the Oculus Quest 2.

Step 2:

Connect your VR headset via a high-speed USB-C cable or wirelessly using tools like Virtual Desktop (for Oculus Quest 2 users).

Step 3:

Ensure that your VR software is up to date and that the Ally X meets the hardware requirements for the VR game or application.

Step 4:

Start your VR game through Steam or other platforms and adjust settings for optimal performance.

3. Optimizing VR Performance To get the best experience, ensure that you:

Keep the refresh rate at a level your GPU can handle.

Reduce visual settings to ensure stable frame rates, as VR gaming requires a high and stable frame rate to prevent motion sickness.

If possible, consider using an eGPU for demanding VR titles to unlock a more immersive and visually appealing VR experience.

Streaming Games from PC (Steam Link, Remote Play, etc.)

Another powerful feature of the ROG Ally X is its ability to stream games from your PC or even other consoles. Using services like Steam Link, NVIDIA GameStream, or Remote Play, you can stream games from a more powerful gaming PC or console directly to your Ally X, allowing you to play high-performance games without straining the handheld's internal hardware.

1. Steam Link Steam Link is a free tool provided by Steam that allows you to stream games from your gaming PC to another device (like the ROG Ally X) over your local network or the internet.

Step 1:

Install Steam on both your gaming PC and the ROG Ally X.

Step 2:

On your Ally X, open Steam and select the game you want to stream from your PC.

Step 3:

Ensure both devices are connected to the same Wi-Fi network for the best performance, or use a wired connection.

Step 4:

Start the stream. The game will run on your gaming PC, but the video and audio will be sent to the Ally X, where you can control the game using Ally's built-in controls.

2. Remote Play (PlayStation and Xbox) Remote Play is another method for streaming games from your PlayStation or Xbox console to the ROG Ally X.

For PlayStation, download the PS Remote Play app and connect to your PS4 or PS5.

For Xbox, use the Xbox app on Windows to stream games from your Xbox Series X|S or Xbox One to Ally X.

3. Optimizing Game Streaming Performance

Use a wired connection for the best performance and lowest latency.

If using Wi-Fi, connect both devices to a 5GHz Wi-Fi network for smoother streaming.

Reduce the stream resolution if you experience lag or stuttering. Most streaming platforms allow you to adjust the stream's resolution based on your network performance.

Connecting Controllers and Peripherals (Wireless/Bluetooth):

The ROG Ally X supports a wide range of external controllers and peripherals, which can be connected either via USB, Bluetooth, or wireless dongles. This opens up a world of possibilities for multiplayer gaming, connecting external keyboards or mice for PC gaming, or simply customizing your control scheme to suit your preferences.

1. Connecting Controllers via Bluetooth Many popular controllers, like the Xbox Series X|S controller or PlayStation DualSense, can be connected to the ROG Ally X wirelessly via Bluetooth.

Step 1:

Open the Bluetooth settings on your Ally X by navigating to Settings > Devices > Bluetooth & other devices.

Step 2:

Put your controller in pairing mode (usually by holding down a specific button combination, such as the Xbox controller's pair button).

Step 3:

Select the controller from the list of available devices on your Ally X and pair it. Once connected, the controller will function just like a standard Xbox controller, and you can use it to play games from Steam, Game Pass, or other platforms.

2. Connecting Controllers via USB If you prefer a wired connection, you can connect a controller directly to the Ally X using a USB-A to USB-C adapter or a USB-C cable. This method ensures zero latency and is great for games where precise control is required.

3. Using Keyboards, Mice, and Other Peripherals The Ally X's USB-C ports also allow you to connect external keyboards, mice, and other peripherals, turning the device into a functional Windows 11 PC. This is particularly useful for productivity tasks, first-person shooters, or strategy games where a mouse and keyboard are preferred.

Simply connect your peripheral via USB or Bluetooth.

You can also use USB-C hubs to connect multiple devices simultaneously, such as a keyboard, mouse, and external storage.

By utilizing these advanced features, the ROG Ally X becomes far more than just a handheld gaming device. Whether you're pushing the limits of graphical performance with an eGPU, stepping into the world of VR, streaming high-end games from your PC, or expanding your control setup with external peripherals, the ROG Ally X is built to handle all your gaming needs with flexibility and power.

Chapter 8.

Display and Audio

The ASUS ROG Ally X is equipped with a powerful display and audio system that ensures an immersive gaming experience. Whether you're adjusting brightness, tweaking color settings, or managing your audio preferences, the device offers a range of customization options to optimize both visual and audio performance for all your gaming and multimedia needs.

Adjusting Display Brightness, Resolution, and Refresh Rate:

The ROG Ally X features a high-quality display designed to provide vivid visuals and smooth frame rates. Knowing how to adjust these settings can help you tailor the experience for different games, battery conservation, or other tasks.

1. Adjusting Brightness Brightness control is essential, especially if you're gaming in different lighting environments.

High brightness can enhance visibility during outdoor use, while reducing brightness can help conserve battery life indoors or during extended play sessions.

Manual Brightness Adjustment:

You can manually adjust brightness from the Windows Quick Settings menu. Simply press Windows + A to open the Action Center, then slide the brightness bar to your desired level.

Automatic Brightness Adjustment:

Windows 11 allows for adaptive brightness that automatically adjusts the screen based on ambient lighting. This feature can be found in Settings > System > Display > Brightness. Enabling this option ensures that your screen remains visible in any environment while conserving battery.

2. Adjusting Resolution The ROG Ally X's display is capable of running at various resolutions, which can be adjusted depending on your preference for gaming performance or battery optimization. A higher resolution like 1080p delivers crisper, more detailed visuals, but it may reduce performance or battery life depending on the game.

Changing Resolution:

Navigate to Settings > System > Display > Scale and Layout to change the resolution. Select your desired resolution from the drop-down list.

For most games, a resolution of 1920x1080 (Full HD) strikes the best balance between performance and visual fidelity.

For less demanding titles, you can lower the resolution to 1280x720 (HD) to improve frame rates and extend battery life.

3. Adjusting Refresh Rate The ROG Ally X supports different refresh rates, which determine how many frames per second (FPS) your display can show. A higher refresh rate like 120Hz provides smoother motion and is perfect for fast-paced games, while lowering it to 60Hz can conserve battery life and reduce heat generation.

Changing Refresh Rate:

To adjust the refresh rate, go to Settings > System > Display > Advanced display settings and choose the desired refresh rate. Some games will automatically adjust the refresh rate for optimal performance, but you can manually switch between modes as needed.

For competitive gaming, set the refresh rate to 120Hz for smoother gameplay.

For casual gaming or everyday use, 60Hz is ideal for saving power without sacrificing much visual quality.

Color Calibration for Optimal Viewing:

For gamers and content creators who are particular about color accuracy, the ROG Ally X provides options for color calibration. Ensuring that colors are accurately represented enhances the visual quality of games, movies, and media content.

1. Accessing Color Calibration Settings Windows 11 has built-in tools for color calibration, which can be accessed via Settings > System > Display > Advanced display settings > Color calibration. This tool guides you through the process of adjusting brightness, contrast, gamma, and color balance to ensure that your display is producing accurate and consistent colors.

2. Custom Color Profiles If you prefer a more vibrant or specific color tone for gaming, you can create custom color

profiles or use pre-calibrated ones provided by ASUS or third-party tools like DisplayCAL. The Armoury Crate software may also include preset color profiles for different game genres, such as FPS mode for sharper contrast or Cinema mode for more saturated colors during movies.

3. External Calibration Tools For professional gamers or content creators, using external hardware calibration tools like the X-Rite i1Display Pro or SpyderX ensures that your display is fine-tuned for the best color accuracy. This is particularly useful if you are using the ROG Ally X for video editing, photography, or content creation, where precise color reproduction is critical.

Managing Audio Settings:

The ROG Ally X is designed with both performance and flexibility in mind when it comes to audio. Whether you are using the built-in speakers or external audio devices, adjusting the audio settings will help you get the best sound quality for gaming, music, or media consumption.

1. Adjusting Volume Levels The volume can be adjusted quickly using the physical volume buttons on the side of the device or through Windows Quick Settings by pressing Windows + A and adjusting the volume slider. For finer control, go to Settings > System > Sound to modify individual

application volumes, such as raising the in-game volume while lowering notifications.

2. Enhancing Audio Quality The ROG Ally X supports Windows Sonic for Headphones and Dolby Atmos, which are spatial sound technologies designed to provide immersive audio. To enable these features, go to Settings > System > Sound > Advanced sound options, then select Spatial sound. These enhancements are particularly beneficial in games with rich soundscapes or directional audio cues.

3. Customizing Audio in Armoury Crate Armoury Crate includes built-in sound profiles that allow you to customize your audio experience based on the type of game you are playing. You can choose from settings like:

FPS Mode:

Enhances environmental sound and footstep clarity.

RPG Mode:

Boosts voice and background music for more immersive storytelling.

Multiplayer Mode:

Emphasizes communication by clarifying dialogue and reducing background noise.

Built-in Speakers Performance:

The ROG Ally X features stereo speakers with Smart Amp technology, designed to deliver clear and punchy audio without distortion, even at higher volumes. While handheld gaming devices aren't typically known for high-quality built-in sound, the Ally X's speakers perform admirably for most gaming and media consumption scenarios.

1. Sound Quality for Gaming The stereo speakers are optimized for gaming, with enough clarity to distinguish key in-game audio cues like enemy footsteps, environmental sounds, and gunfire. The soundstage, while not as expansive as that of external speakers or headphones, provides sufficient immersion for portable gaming.

2. Volume and Bass Output The speakers have good volume levels for casual use but may lack deep bass, which is expected from a device of this size. For action-packed games, you may want to use headphones or external speakers for a fuller audio experience.

3. Speaker Placement The placement of the speakers along the sides of the device ensures that sound isn't blocked by your hands during gaming sessions, which can be a common issue in handheld gaming consoles. This strategic positioning helps maintain audio clarity and directionality.

External Audio Devices (Headsets and Speakers):

For a more immersive and high-quality audio experience, the ROG Ally X supports a variety of external audio devices, including both wired and wireless headphones, Bluetooth speakers, and USB-C audio devices.

1. Connecting Wired Headsets The ROG Ally X includes a 3.5mm headphone jack, allowing you to connect your favorite gaming headset or earbuds for direct audio output. Wired connections offer low-latency audio, which is essential for competitive gaming or media editing. Simply plug in your headset, and the device will automatically switch to headset mode.

2. Using Bluetooth Headphones If you prefer a wireless experience, the Ally X's Bluetooth 5.2 capabilities allow

seamless pairing with a variety of Bluetooth headphones, headsets, and speakers.

To pair a device, go to Settings > Bluetooth & devices and select Add Bluetooth device.

Once connected, you can enjoy wireless audio with minimal latency, although it's recommended to use aptX or LDAC-compatible headphones for the best sound quality and low latency.

3. USB-C Audio Devices The ROG Ally X also supports USB-C audio devices, such as high-fidelity DACs (Digital-to-Analog Converters) and USB-C headphones. This allows audiophiles to use high-resolution audio equipment with the Ally X, delivering superior sound quality compared to standard Bluetooth or 3.5mm outputs.

4. External Speakers If you prefer external speakers for a more robust audio setup, you can connect the ROG Ally X to Bluetooth speakers or wired speakers via the 3.5mm jack or USB-C. This is ideal for gaming at home, watching movies, or using the Ally X as a mini-PC for media streaming.

In conclusion, the ROG Ally X excels in providing customizable display and audio options that enhance both gaming and multimedia experiences. Whether you're adjusting brightness, optimizing color settings, managing your audio preferences, or using external devices, the Ally X ensures that you have full control over your visual and auditory environment, making every game and movie more immersive.

Chapter 9.

Battery Optimization and Thermal Management

The ASUS ROG Ally X is a powerful handheld gaming device designed to deliver desktop-level performance in a portable form factor. With its high-end components, it's important to manage battery life and control thermals efficiently to get the best performance and longevity out of the device. This section will guide you through strategies for optimizing power consumption, switching between power profiles, understanding the cooling system, and managing fan speed and temperature.

Managing Power Consumption:

Battery life is always a crucial consideration for handheld gaming devices, especially when playing demanding AAA titles. The ROG Ally X offers several ways to manage power consumption and prolong battery life without significantly sacrificing performance.

1. Lowering Display Brightness One of the simplest ways to conserve battery life is by lowering the display brightness. High brightness levels consume more power, so reducing the screen brightness when playing indoors or in low-light conditions can significantly extend battery life.

You can adjust brightness in the Windows Quick Settings by pressing Windows + A and using the brightness slider.

2. Using Power Saver Mode Windows 11 has a built-in Power Saver mode, which limits background activities and reduces performance slightly to conserve power. This mode is especially useful when you're browsing the web, watching videos, or playing less demanding games. You can enable it by going to Settings > System > Power & battery, then selecting Power Saver under Battery mode.

3. Disabling Unused Features Turning off unused features such as Bluetooth, Wi-Fi, and RGB lighting when they aren't needed can save battery life. For instance, if you're playing an offline game, disabling Wi-Fi can prevent unnecessary background processes from draining the battery.

4. Limiting Background Applications Minimizing the number of active applications running in the background can help save battery life. Close any unnecessary apps by pressing Ctrl +

Shift + Esc to open the Task Manager and stop processes that aren't needed for gaming.

Switching Between Power Profiles:

The ASUS ROG Ally X features multiple power profiles, each designed to balance performance and battery life for different use cases. These profiles allow you to switch between low-power settings for casual tasks and high-performance modes for gaming.

1. 13W Power Mode (Low Power) The 13W Power Mode is ideal for less demanding games or casual tasks such as web browsing, media playback, or light gaming. This mode conserves battery life by limiting the device's power draw, which in turn generates less heat and reduces fan noise.

Use this mode when gaming on the go and when battery longevity is a priority over peak performance.

2. 17W Power Mode (Balanced) The 17W Power Mode provides a balanced approach between performance and battery life. This mode is ideal for moderate gaming sessions where you still want smooth gameplay but need to preserve battery life for extended playtime.

It's the perfect option for titles that don't require maximum performance but still benefit from some additional power over the 13W mode.

3. 25W Power Mode (High Performance) The 25W Power Mode is the high-performance setting intended for more graphically intensive games. This mode unlocks the full potential of the ROG Ally X, delivering the highest possible frame rates and performance at the expense of battery life.

Use this mode when plugged into an external power source or for shorter gaming sessions when maximum performance is necessary. Be mindful that using this mode for extended periods will drain the battery quickly and may cause the device to heat up more rapidly.

4. Custom Power Profiles in Armoury Crate Armoury Crate allows you to create custom power profiles, giving you more control over CPU, GPU, and fan speeds. You can fine-tune these settings based on the specific game you are playing or the task you are performing, balancing power usage and performance to suit your needs.

Cooling System Overview:

The ASUS ROG Ally X features an advanced cooling system designed to manage the heat generated by the powerful internal components. It uses a combination of liquid metal thermal compound and efficient dual-fan cooling to keep temperatures under control, ensuring smooth performance even during extended gaming sessions.

1. Liquid Metal Thermal Compound One of the standout features of the ROG Ally X is the use of liquid metal on the CPU, which significantly improves thermal conductivity compared to traditional thermal paste. This helps keep the processor cooler under heavy loads, preventing thermal throttling and maintaining performance during long gaming sessions.

2. Dual-Fan Cooling System The device is equipped with a dual-fan cooling system that efficiently expels heat through strategically placed vents. This design ensures that hot air is quickly expelled from the device, allowing cooler air to circulate and prevent overheating.

The cooling system is designed to operate quietly, even when the fans are running at higher speeds, so you can enjoy immersive gaming without being distracted by fan noise.

3. Heat Dissipation and Vents The heat dissipation design of the ROG Ally X includes several intake and exhaust vents located on the sides and back of the device. These vents are crucial in maintaining airflow, allowing the internal components to stay cool during intensive gaming sessions.

Fan Speed Control and Temperature Monitoring:

To ensure your device runs optimally, the ROG Ally X allows you to adjust fan speed and monitor temperatures in real-time. This helps you manage thermal performance, especially during demanding tasks like gaming, where the device generates the most heat.

1. Fan Speed Control The fan speed can be manually adjusted through Armoury Crate to suit your preferences. If you're focused on performance, you can set the fans to run at higher speeds, keeping the device cool while gaming. Conversely, if you're performing lighter tasks and prefer a quieter experience, you can lower the fan speed.

Auto Mode:

This setting automatically adjusts fan speeds based on the current thermal load.

Silent Mode:

Prioritizes quieter fan operation, sacrificing some cooling efficiency.

Turbo Mode:

Maximizes cooling efficiency by running the fans at full speed to prevent any thermal throttling during heavy gaming.

2. Temperature Monitoring Real-time temperature monitoring is essential for keeping track of the device's internal thermals. Through Armoury Crate, you can view temperature readings for both the CPU and GPU to ensure they remain within safe operating limits.

Normal Temperatures:

Under moderate load, temperatures should generally remain around 60°C to 75°C for the CPU and GPU.

High Temperatures:

During intense gaming, temperatures may rise to 85°C or slightly higher. The cooling system will work to keep temperatures from exceeding this range, but you may experience thermal throttling if the device is pushed to its limits for extended periods.

If temperatures consistently run too high, consider increasing the fan speed or taking breaks to let the device cool down.

3. Optimizing for Longevity Running your device at lower temperatures extends the longevity of the internal components. By managing fan speed and thermal settings properly, you can prevent unnecessary wear and tear on the CPU and GPU, ensuring your ROG Ally X continues to perform well over time.

Conclusion:

Effective battery optimization and thermal management are key to getting the most out of your ASUS ROG Ally X. By switching between power profiles, adjusting fan speeds, and managing temperatures, you can ensure that your device delivers peak performance without overheating or draining the battery too quickly. Whether you're playing AAA games, streaming content, or performing everyday tasks, these tools give you full control over power consumption and thermal performance, maximizing both the efficiency and longevity of your gaming experience.

Chapter 10.

Maintenance and Troubleshooting

Maintaining your ASUS ROG Ally X and addressing common issues are critical for ensuring the longevity and smooth operation of the device. In this chapter, we will cover some of the most common problems that users might face and provide detailed instructions on how to fix them. We will also discuss the importance of regular maintenance, including software updates, cleaning, and care for your handheld console.

Common Issues and Fixes:

While the ASUS ROG Ally X is designed to offer high performance, users may occasionally experience issues. Below are the most frequently encountered problems and solutions to address them:

Overheating:

Overheating is a common issue, especially when running resource-intensive games or applications. If your device becomes too hot, it can lead to performance drops, uncomfortable handling, or even hardware damage if left unchecked.

1. Causes of Overheating:

Running the device at maximum performance settings for extended periods.

Poor ventilation due to blocked air vents.

Ambient temperature being too high, making it difficult for the device to cool.

2. Solutions:

Adjust Power Profiles:

Switch to a lower power profile like 13W or 17W mode when you're not playing demanding games. This will reduce heat generation.

Optimize Cooling:

Ensure the air vents are not obstructed. Place the device on a flat surface that allows airflow.

Use a Cooling Pad or External Fan:

If you often game for extended periods, an external cooling pad can help dissipate heat more efficiently.

Keep Software Updated:

Firmware and software updates often include thermal management improvements. Ensure your device is up to date.

Freezing or Lagging:

Lagging, stuttering, or freezing can occur due to various reasons, such as software glitches, insufficient memory, or high system resource usage.

1. Causes of Freezing:

Too many apps running in the background, consuming RAM and CPU.

Corrupt or outdated software and drivers.

Insufficient cooling, causing thermal throttling.

2. Solutions:

Close Background Applications:

Open Task Manager by pressing Ctrl + Shift + Esc and close any unnecessary processes.

Update Drivers and Firmware:

Ensure your GPU and other system drivers are updated. These updates often address performance bottlenecks.

Lower In-Game Settings:

If a game is too resource-intensive, try lowering its graphical settings to reduce the load on the GPU and CPU.

Check for Malware:

Use Windows Defender or a trusted third-party antivirus to scan for malware that might be causing system slowdowns.

SD Card Slot Issues:

The SD card slot is essential for expanding the storage of the ROG Ally X, but users might encounter issues such as the card not being recognized or slow read/write speeds.

1. Causes of SD Card Slot Issues:

Incompatible or damaged SD card.

Improper insertion of the SD card.

Dust or debris in the slot causing poor connectivity.

2. Solutions:

Check SD Card Compatibility:

Ensure that the SD card meets the device's specifications (e.g., UHS-I or UHS-II speed class).

Reinsert the Card:

Carefully remove and reinsert the SD card, making sure it clicks into place.

Check for Debris:

Gently clean the SD card slot with a can of compressed air to remove any dust or debris.

Format the SD Card:

If the card is not recognized, try formatting it using a PC before reinserting it into the device. Ensure that you back up important data before formatting.

Updating BIOS and System Drivers:

Keeping your device's BIOS and system drivers up to date is critical for optimal performance, stability, and compatibility with new games and applications.

1. How to Update BIOS:

Visit the official ASUS Support website and search for the ROG Ally X model.

Download the latest BIOS update from the support page.

Place the BIOS file on a USB drive, plug it into the device, and follow the instructions in the BIOS update menu, accessible through the startup screen.

2. Updating Drivers:

Open Armoury Crate and check for any driver updates specific to your device.

You can also update Windows drivers by going to Device Manager, right-clicking the hardware you want to update, and selecting Update Driver.

3. Automatic Updates:

Enable Windows Update and Armoury Crate auto-updates to ensure your system is always running the latest software.

Factory Reset Instructions:

In some cases, the only way to resolve persistent issues is to perform a factory reset. This will restore your ROG Ally X to its original settings, erasing all data on the device, so make sure to back up any important files before proceeding.

1. Backup Your Data:

Save all important files to an external drive or cloud service before starting the reset process.

2. Performing a Factory Reset:

Open the Start Menu, select Settings, and navigate to System > Recovery.

Under Reset this PC, select Get Started.

Choose whether you want to keep your files or remove everything.

Follow the on-screen instructions to complete the factory reset. The device will restart several times during the process.

Cleaning and Care for the Device:

Regular cleaning and proper care will keep your ROG Ally X in top condition and prevent issues caused by dust buildup or improper handling.

1. Cleaning the Screen:

Use a microfiber cloth to wipe the display and remove fingerprints or smudges.

Avoid using harsh chemicals. Instead, use a screen cleaning solution designed for electronics.

2. Cleaning Vents and Ports:

Over time, dust can accumulate in the vents and ports, restricting airflow and causing overheating.

Use a can of compressed air to clean out dust from the vents and ports, making sure to do this in a well-ventilated area.

Avoid using any sharp objects to clean the ports, as this may damage the connectors.

3. Battery Care:

Avoid leaving your device plugged in continuously, as this can reduce the overall battery lifespan.

Try to keep the battery level between 20% and 80% for optimal longevity.

When storing the device for long periods, ensure it's at around 50% charge to prevent battery degradation.

4. Protecting the Device:

Use a protective case when traveling with the ROG Ally X to prevent scratches, dents, or other physical damage.

Keep the device away from extreme temperatures, moisture, or direct sunlight, which could damage internal components.

Conclusion:

Proper maintenance and troubleshooting are essential to ensure the longevity and smooth functioning of your ASUS ROG Ally X. By following the steps outlined in this chapter, you can address common issues, keep your system up to date, and maintain the hardware in optimal condition. Regularly cleaning and updating your device, as well as properly managing its power and thermal settings, will ensure that your gaming experience remains enjoyable and hassle-free for years to come.

Chapter 11.

Frequently Asked Questions (FAQ)

In this chapter, we address some of the most common questions that users have regarding the ASUS ROG Ally X. Whether you're looking for general troubleshooting advice, tips on performance optimization, or answers to battery and charging concerns, this FAQ section is designed to provide clear and actionable information to help you get the most out of your device.

General Troubleshooting Tips:

This section covers some basic troubleshooting steps that can resolve most minor issues you might encounter while using the ASUS ROG Ally X.

1. My ROG Ally X is not turning on. What should I do?

First, make sure the device is charged. Plug it into a power source using the provided charger and check if the charging indicator lights up.

If the device is fully charged and still not turning on, perform a soft reset by holding down the Power button for 10-15 seconds. This forces the device to restart.

If the soft reset does not work, try connecting the device to a different power outlet or using a different USB-C charging cable.

2. How do I fix a frozen or unresponsive screen?

Press and hold the Power button for about 10-15 seconds to force a shutdown. After a few seconds, turn the device back on by pressing the Power button again.

If the issue persists, consider performing a factory reset (see Chapter 11 for detailed instructions). Remember to back up your data before doing so.

3. Why is my ROG Ally X running slowly or lagging?

Close Background Apps:

Open the Task Manager by pressing Ctrl + Shift + Esc, and close any unnecessary applications that might be consuming system resources.

Check for Software Updates:

Ensure your Windows system and drivers are up to date. Outdated software can sometimes cause performance bottlenecks.

Adjust Power Profiles:

If you're gaming, ensure that the device is set to a higher power profile, such as 25W mode, for maximum performance.

Performance Optimization FAQ:

Ensuring optimal performance while gaming or using resource-intensive applications is key to getting the best experience on your ROG Ally X. Below are some common performance-related questions and their solutions.

1. How can I improve my gaming performance on the ROG Ally X?

Use Performance Mode:

Switch to Performance Mode in Armoury Crate to unlock the device's full potential. You can choose between power profiles (13W, 17W, or 25W) depending on the balance between battery life and performance that you want.

Lower Graphics Settings:

If a game is not running smoothly, try lowering the graphics settings within the game itself (e.g., reducing resolution, disabling high-level shadows, etc.).

Update Game and System Drivers:

Regularly updating both your games and the system's drivers ensures you're getting the latest performance optimizations.

2. How can I manage overheating during extended gaming sessions?

Use a Cooling Pad:

If you're gaming for long periods, consider using a cooling pad to help maintain lower temperatures.

Limit Background Apps:

Close any applications running in the background that aren't necessary. This helps to reduce the load on the CPU and GPU, leading to less heat generation.

Set Fan Speed:

Within Armoury Crate, you can manually adjust the fan speed to improve cooling. Setting the fans to a higher speed during intense gaming sessions can prevent overheating.

3. Why is my ROG Ally X lagging during gameplay even on high performance settings?

Check for Thermal Throttling:

High temperatures can cause the device to throttle performance to prevent overheating. Monitor the temperatures using software like Armoury Crate. If the CPU or GPU temperatures are high, improve cooling conditions by ensuring good airflow or using an external cooling solution.

Free Up Storage:

Low available storage can also impact performance. Consider clearing unnecessary files or expanding your storage with an SD card or by upgrading the internal SSD.

4. What is the best resolution and refresh rate for gaming?

Native Resolution:

The ROG Ally X's display supports a maximum resolution of 1920x1080 (Full HD). This provides the best clarity and detail for gaming.

Refresh Rate:

A refresh rate of 120Hz is ideal for most fast-paced games, as it delivers smoother visuals. However, for more power-efficient gaming or less demanding titles, you can reduce the refresh rate to 60Hz to conserve battery life.

Battery Life and Charging Questions:

Battery life and power management are key concerns for handheld gaming consoles like the ROG Ally X. Here are answers to some of the most common battery and charging questions.

1. How long does the battery last during gaming sessions?

Battery life depends on the power profile and the intensity of the games being played. On average:

In 13W mode (low power), expect about 5-7 hours of battery life for less demanding games or general usage.

In 17W mode (balanced performance), expect around 3-4 hours of gaming.

In 25W mode (high performance), expect around 2-3 hours for the most demanding titles.

Reducing screen brightness and limiting background apps can also extend battery life.

2. How do I charge the ROG Ally X, and how long does it take?

Use the included USB-C charger to charge your device. It takes approximately 2 hours to fully charge the ROG Ally X from 0% to 100% when using the provided fast charger.

Tip: Always use an official or high-quality third-party USB-C charger that supports Power Delivery (PD) to ensure safe and efficient charging.

3. Can I play games while charging the ROG Ally X?

Yes, you can use the ROG Ally X while it's charging. However, it's important to note that running intensive games while charging can generate more heat, which may cause the device to throttle performance.

For the best experience while charging, play in 17W mode, which balances battery charging and gaming performance. If you experience overheating, consider reducing your power profile or limiting intensive tasks.

4. What are the best practices for maximizing battery life?

Use Lower Power Profiles for Less Demanding Tasks:

If you're browsing the web or watching videos, use the 13W mode to conserve battery life.

Disable RGB Lighting:

The customizable RGB lighting can consume battery power. If you're looking to extend battery life, disable or reduce the brightness of these lights through the Armoury Crate software.

Reduce Screen Brightness:

Dimming the display can significantly improve battery life during extended gaming sessions.

Switch to Lower Refresh Rates:

Set the screen refresh rate to 60Hz instead of 120Hz if you're not playing fast-paced games. This can also extend battery life.

5. Why is my battery draining so quickly even in low power mode?

Check Background Applications:

Open Task Manager to identify apps running in the background that are consuming resources. Close any unnecessary programs to conserve battery.

Power Profiles:

Make sure you're using the correct power profile for your current activities. Even in low power mode, running resource-intensive games or apps can drain the battery faster than expected.

Update Firmware:

Battery optimizations are often included in firmware updates. Make sure that your device's firmware and software are up to date to improve battery management.

6. How can I check my battery health?

You can check your battery health status in Windows 11. Go to Settings > System > Battery, and you'll see your device's current battery capacity compared to its original design capacity.

Additionally, you can use third-party software tools to monitor more detailed battery health metrics, such as the number of charge cycles and current battery wear.

Conclusion:

This FAQ chapter provides essential troubleshooting and optimization tips for the ASUS ROG Ally X, ensuring that you can resolve common issues and enhance your device's performance. Whether you're optimizing battery life, fine-tuning game settings, or addressing technical issues, following these guidelines will help you maximize the potential of your handheld gaming console for a seamless gaming experience.

Chapter 12.

Warranty and Support

In this chapter, we cover essential information about the warranty and support services for your ASUS ROG Ally X. Whether you need assistance with a malfunction, have questions about repairs or replacements, or simply want to understand your device's warranty coverage, this section is here to guide you through the process.

Warranty Information:

ASUS provides a standard warranty for the ROG Ally X, which covers defects in material and workmanship under normal use. However, it is important to understand the specific terms and conditions of your warranty to ensure you are fully covered.

1. Warranty Coverage:

Standard Warranty:

Your ROG Ally X typically comes with a 1-year warranty from the date of purchase, but the length of coverage can vary depending on the region and retailer. Some regions may offer extended warranties or promotional extended coverage at the time of purchase.

What's Covered:

The warranty covers hardware defects and malfunctions under normal usage. If any internal component fails due to a manufacturing defect, ASUS will repair or replace the affected parts.

What's Not Covered:

The warranty does not cover issues caused by user misuse, accidents, water damage, unauthorized repairs or modifications, or wear and tear from normal use. Additionally, damages due to external devices or peripherals (e.g., chargers, batteries, etc.) may not be covered unless specified by ASUS.

Battery Coverage:

The warranty typically covers defects in battery performance for the first year of ownership, but if the battery's performance deteriorates due to aging (which is a natural process), it may not be eligible for warranty service after the first year.

2. How to Register Your Product:

It's recommended to register your ROG Ally X on the ASUS website to ensure your device is officially covered under the warranty. Registration can also streamline the process in case you need to claim warranty services.

Visit the ASUS support website and create an account or log in. Then, navigate to the Product Registration page and enter the necessary details such as the device's serial number, purchase date, and location of purchase.

3. Warranty Extensions:

Depending on your region, ASUS may offer extended warranty plans for an additional cost. These plans can extend your warranty beyond the standard one-year period and provide additional coverage, including protection against accidental damage.

Check with the retailer or ASUS support to see if extended warranty plans are available.

Contacting ASUS Support:

If you need assistance with your ROG Ally X, contacting ASUS support is an essential step. Whether you have a technical issue, need advice, or require a repair, ASUS offers several ways to get in touch with their customer service team.

1. ASUS Support Website:

The first step in troubleshooting any issues with your device is to visit the ASUS support website. Here, you can access resources such as product manuals, FAQs, and troubleshooting guides.

Visit the support page at https://www.asus.com/support and search for your device model to find specific resources related to the ROG Ally X.

2. Online Chat:

ASUS offers an online chat service that allows you to get real-time support from a customer service representative. This option is useful for general inquiries and minor troubleshooting issues.

On the ASUS support website, navigate to the Contact Us section and select the Live Chat option. You will be connected with a support agent who can guide you through potential solutions or provide further assistance.

3. Email Support:

If you prefer written communication or your issue requires detailed information, you can contact ASUS via email. The support team typically responds within 24-48 hours.

Email support can be accessed through the Contact Us section of the ASUS support website. Choose the appropriate email option and provide a detailed description of your issue.

4. Phone Support:

If you need to speak with a support representative directly, ASUS provides customer support via phone. This is the best option for urgent issues that may require immediate attention.

Phone numbers vary by region, so visit the Contact Us page of the ASUS support website to find the phone number specific to your country or region.

5. Social Media Support:

ASUS is active on various social media platforms, including Twitter and Facebook, where you can direct message them for support inquiries. While this option may not be as immediate as phone or live chat support, it's an alternative way to reach out.

Repair and Replacement Procedures:

If your ROG Ally X requires repair or replacement, understanding the procedures will help you navigate the process smoothly.

1. Identifying the Issue:

Before contacting ASUS for repair, perform basic troubleshooting steps as outlined in the Troubleshooting FAQ section of this guide. This can help you determine whether the issue is a simple software glitch, a battery-related problem, or a more serious hardware issue.

If the issue persists after troubleshooting, gather as much information as possible about the problem. This includes:

A clear description of the issue.

Steps that trigger the problem.

Error messages or codes, if applicable.

System information such as OS version, RAM, and storage details.

2. Requesting Repair:

Once you've identified the problem and contacted ASUS support, the next step is to request a repair or replacement. If your device is still under warranty, ASUS will typically cover the cost of repairs.

Depending on the nature of the issue, ASUS may offer several options for resolution:

Repair:

If the issue is related to hardware, ASUS may request that you send your device to an authorized service center for repairs. ASUS will provide you with a shipping label and instructions on how to send your device.

Replacement:

If your device is beyond repair or has a critical failure, ASUS may offer a replacement. If you qualify for a replacement under warranty, ASUS will send you a new or refurbished unit.

3. Repair Service Centers:

ASUS has a network of authorized service centers where your device can be sent for repairs. These centers are equipped to handle most common issues, including screen replacements, battery issues, and motherboard failures.

Before sending your device for repair, ensure you back up all your data, as repairs may require factory resetting the device, which can erase all personal files.

4. Return and Refund Policies:

If your device is still within the return window (usually 30 days from the purchase date), you may be eligible for a refund or exchange through the retailer where you purchased the device. In some cases, ASUS may also handle returns directly.

To request a refund or return, contact the retailer or ASUS support for instructions. Keep your proof of purchase handy, as you'll likely need it to process the return.

5. Out-of-Warranty Repairs:

If your ROG Ally X is out of warranty or if the issue is not covered under warranty, ASUS may still offer repair services for a fee. In this case, you will be informed of the estimated cost for repairs before any work is performed.

You may also explore third-party repair services, but keep in mind that using unauthorized repair centers may void any remaining warranty on your device.

Conclusion:

Understanding the warranty coverage, how to contact ASUS support, and the repair and replacement procedures is essential to ensure that you can quickly and efficiently resolve any issues with your ROG Ally X. By familiarizing yourself with these processes, you can minimize downtime and get your device back in working order as soon as possible. Whether your issue is covered under warranty or requires out-of-pocket repair, knowing how to navigate the ASUS support system ensures that you are always prepared.